Creations of Little Janie, The Life Inside a Mirror

Creations of Little Tanie, The Life Inside a Mirror

A Virtual Presence, An Existence Beyond

Tanmeyta Darshee Yashman "Darshika"

PARTRIDGE

A Penguin Random House Company

To order additional copies of this book, contact
Partridge India
000 800 10062 62
www.partridgepublishing.com/india
orders.india@partridgepublishing.com

My Premier Edition.
The first Volume ever

"Fortune comes once and it comes by Chance !! But *Fruits come many a times and they come by Practice! So, keep Practicing . . . . without waiting for a Chance !!" as taught by my Guide (Guru ji) Pandit Shree Niwas Tiwari 'Aazaad'

*Good results = Success

Overview

The eccentric, mysterious nature is found very obvious in each of the creation; every bit of the poems . . . . word by word, an unveiling magic.

Just as a dip in a vast ocean, the poems leave a deep impact and long lasting impression . . removing stress and rejeuvenating the inner most spirit.

The nature of poems being versatile and diverse, the author prevents exaustion, boredom or monotonous fatigue.

Each poem soothes and relieves. It calms the senses to bring out the peace in oneself.

Some dont make a direct meaning. Some sound crazy, yet all of the poems bring pleasure and joy to every age group.

Created passionately, by a passionate being, the poetry collection aims at reviving creativity in readers.

A verbal expedition commences to enhance the volume of life, adding substance to it.

Prayer

Asking for Blessings

In the first page of this book, I express respect to God, in order to receive blessings that I would require to commence a new journey of precious learning process and my very own creations.

I bow down to the Almighty and pay tribute to His kindness, mercy and generosity.

I also kneel down to ask for God's sacred powers that should act as a source of teachings and a guiding force through my difficulties and tough ways; the rough paths.

Dear God,

Please do accept my prayer and regard.

Guide me in my routes. Your guidance is of utmost importance; a driving spirit behind my journey I begin with, now.

Bless Me!

Acknowledgement

I want to thank my my parents Sumit Singh and Saaki, for their ever spiritual presence, motivating me. They've been an inspiration to me to write.

My grandmother, Rekha Prasad and my spiritual guide, Pt. Shree Niwas Tiwari "Aazaad" are to be thanked for being a source of encouragement.

A little "thank you" note for my sweet neighbours, The Rai family which includes Divya Rai, Pankaj Rai and Abhinav Rai.

Not to forget Kanchan Tripathi, my grandmother's research scholar who has been staying with us for a while now and been affectionate and kind like an aunt.

I'm also thankful to each of my friends to keep me bubbling with ideas.

Since I've been a patient for a while, I express gratification to all the doctors who've restructured me.

Above all, I want to thank the Almighty with the following letter.

Dear Good Lord,

You have blessed me with more than I asked for, deserved and expected.

I run short of words . . to express gratitude dear lord.

Thank you for everything I can count on today . . . ,
in form of holy ~ divine ~ sacred gifts that you have
blessed me with.

Thanks a lot ☺

Dedications

I dedicate my writings to my great grandmothers, Laxmi Devi Saxena and Vimla Singh. My grandparents, Surendra Kanwar Saxena, Satish Kumar Singh and Manorma Devi. My uncles, Sarabjit Kahlon, Tajinder Singh and Prabh Kahlon. My great grandfathers, Late Shyam Babu Saxena and Devi Shankar Singh above everyone, as he has been an English scholar, Masters in English and a retired School Principal.

Dedicating to the Super Energies

I dedicate to God and the holy ~ sacred ~ divine powers to have graced this book with my writings, my words, my learning and my thoughts.

I dedicate my creativity to my great grandmother Mrs. Lalita Prasad, a lady who could motivate eight children of hers to stand on their own via high education, when she herself was not prividged to have availed the same.

Hi am Saaki. I live at 31 Shubham Apts, Naria, Varanasi, UP, India but I presume myself to be daughter of Saaki whose name is Tanmeyta who's from C-24/47, near Piplani Katra, Kabir Chaura, Varanasi, UP, India

Introductory Poem

"Smiles brought by friends and family,
helping to come back"

Hello World, I'm back again
Tearing away the gloom and pain,
I'm back once again
I chase my dreams, locked inside
Smiling sweet times are stored in pride
Pride is in friends and family
Love makes us smile prettily
It's important to love, it's necessary to smile
Smiles confirm of a mind that is fertile
Love can conquer hearts and minds
Love is a crown which a princess finds
Pride is in friends and family
Love makes us smile prettily
It's important to love, it's necessary to smile
Smiles confirm of a mind that is fertile
This beauty that I create, comes from the beauty within me
The beauty of love, love for my family
Life takes leaps, jumps from a point to another
Life guides us always, like a caring mother
I could be incorrect, I may be right
As long as I live, I have to fight
Fight my own battle, discover myself
Only then can I find sunshine bright

It's important to love, it's necessary to smile

Smiles confirm of a mind that is fertile

Love can conquer hearts and minds

Love is a crown which a princess finds

Section 1

Ocean of Wisdom

Tanie's Rhymes

Poem no. 1

Nature is a poetry in itself . . it Inspires

From behind the curtain of clouds,
The Sun took a glimpse of us all with a wink
A poem filled the sky
Its words spread before I could think
Mind began to explore records
Its chain opened like a link
Nature smiled back to the surrounding
The sky ran shy with a blushing pink
From behind the curtain of clouds,
The Sun glanced at the world, with a wink

Poem no. 2

Fresh Start, New Beginning . .
. . Panache Day . . Every Day !!

A network of moments, life is a mesh
Every morning we must start fresh
Each single day to commence with a brand new thresh
As we begin yet another day
Accidental incidences must not replay
The ills that took place, must be eliminated from mind
The unfavourable that occurred must be eradicated from kind
Thus we create a panache history
Novel be . . the entire inventory
That is how we learn arbitrary

Poem no. 3

Pack off Lazy bones . .
No Time to Waste

Misty breeze
Snoring Sun
Winky Moon
So much fun
Sleep must be packed up
Exercise must be done
Speeding day is on the run

Poem no. 4

To my Folks . . I can't bid Goodbye

A red ribbon bow
Something I'd always wish to buy
I'd be on my toe
if ever I'm shy
Even when I'd be unable to become a pro
I shall never lie
Raised eyebrow
is of a clever guy
To such a cunning foe
I must hardly reply
With someone innocent as a doe
I must never play a sly
Tears flow
Thoughts fly
Feelings show
when I try
If my loved ones go
I'd simply die
They are the people
I cannot bid goodbye !

Poem no. 5

A whole story . . on the ceiling called Sky

I notice the hue
of an amazing blue
as I sit under a clear sky
Mind begins to wander
Thoughts begin to fly
Someone special, whose face I drew
On the blue ceiling
with a deep sigh
Wandering mind begins to wonder
that I must be on the review
Thoughts start planning
how must I
I aim at being honest and true
and aspire to reach up high
Soothing hue of an amazing blue
I write a whole story in the depth of the sky !

Poem no. 6

Continuity of Life
Ever Forward

Into a beautiful day
Every move we make

Towards our missions and ambitions
Careful steps we take

The continuity of life
Without a sudden break

Ever forward
For heaven's sake

If ever at pause
Living shall shake

While making sure
To stay away from a world of fantasy
I pinch myself to feel awake

Ignoring all the whims and fancies
From sweet dream I wake

Coming back from a wonder land
Certainly gives heart an ache

Yet one has to face reality
And prevent from making mistake

A product must always be of utility
What so ever be the intake

Poem no. 7

Try and Win

Often I felt
That I was alone

A wayless route . . I was shown

Yet something would shake me from within
It told me . . how I must try and win
To prove the worth of my family kin

Poem no. 8

Gladness . . At no one's stake

I wonder if Adam was a boat
And Eve was his lake

How do we come to know
If a person is fake

I think the one would be
Curvy in movement
And sleazy as snake

A coin of livelihood
For a slice of joy like a gold flake

Gladness is an icing on a "merry time" cake

Why to forgo them
At someone else's stake

Poem no. 9 a)

Unity in Diversity

A force in oneself,
every human being out sources

Unity be . . the diverse forces
Unity matters the most
Unification brings forth, a strong host
It also encourages Universal brotherhood
Practicing peace and patience
that one always should
Also tolerance to one another's views
as we would
We need to be cordial and co operative
To do our society good
It is the right of each one of us
to be heard and understood

Poem no. 9 b)

Something sweet

Touch elders' feet
Then take a seat
For one is to meet and greet
And not just eat
Now that is sweet
That is the way,
Super stars beat !

Poem no. 10

Nature .. an ever Inspiration

From beneath the cover of petals
a rose bud innocently smiled

It greeted its surrounding with a lively spirit
Seemed like a mother stroking her child

Vibrant as a rainbow
Flamboyant as a butterfly
The environment went colourfully wild

Yet it knew .. till where to mark
And remained soothingly mild

I gathered all my productive thoughts
And had them collectively compiled

Nature being an ever inspiration,
the poetry got marvellously styled

Poem no. 11

"Cloudy Sky" on a foggy day . .
. . with fuming thoughts

Within the ceiling of sky, the clouds made shape on an oak

In a garden of choices, the lanes appeared like a fork

On a misty day, the surrounding looked like smoke

With sentimental gestures, the friends seemed to poke

Warriors were the ones, whose hearts never broke

Dreams came crashing, when an imaginative person woke

Honey seemed to shower, when a princess spoke

Fools are the ones, who give prior importance to cloak

In the sunset sky, the golden ball were to soak

Poem no. 12

Sprite .. like a "Candle Light"

I walked a path
That wasn't much known to me

I couldn't have appreciation for
A route that was shown to me

From curiosity that had grown inside
A sparkling star had shown beside

It was something
For which I would've died

Desires fly in the sky, like a kite
The string of which should be under control, in spite

Desperations grew out of my greatest smite
Soon I found a smiling sprite
The sprite guided me through the path,
Amidst all the despite

The Angel appeared like a candle light

Poem no. 13

A poetry formed . . . . "Hap Hazard" !!

In the magical land of words
Words scattered in the sky like flying birds

A flock of sentiments
in heaps or herds

its frequency so high
in multi mega hertz

A mindless thought
like that of a nerd's

A form not clear,
sounding of an absurd's

A poetry formed in hap hazard's

I wonder if it's a product
of some haggard's

Words flow out
as that of a wizard's

Poem no. 14

I tried my best . .
to answer my whys

Life seems like a test
to bring out from me, the best
Snatching all that I believed
my rivals seemed relieved
Still I tried my best
To retain my zeal and zest
Sometimes a bit of anger I threw
Living suppressed was not to continue
My aim was not to create terror
Nor was it, to be an emperor
I just needed to answer my whys
that could cover my silly little lies

Poem no. 15

Tearing away .. Ignorance

Put forth, the best you've got
Life is but too short
Do what you can .. on your part
The work you do .. must be smart
Things must be done .. straight from heart
Tearing away .. the smoke of ignorance
Wisdom must be achieved .. in abundance
Knowledge being .. the only route to success
Else one cant have a wordly access

Poem no. 16

Morning glory brings Delight !

Ever so cheerful . . the morning sight
Morning glory . . brings delight
In the presence of God, one builds insight
And wishes the Sun, to keep shining bright
Life is a struggle, living is a fight
Strength comes from encouragement
When dear ones hug close and tight
Morning is the time, for the mind to take a flight
Passions grow, thoughts ignite
Morning glory brings delight
Why have fear, we must remove fright
Ever be . . good experience to invite

Poem no. 17

World salutes . . . . Happening Guy

Come on friends . . we can try
Not to stay shut . . I tell you why
The world salutes a happening guy
People bow down . . to a stature that's high
In every field, conditions imply
To be in moderation, and not turn fly
We must open up, and not be shy
The world salutes . . a happening guy
Who has moist speech, and never dry

Poem no. 18

Life is a Ceremony

Every day we move step by step
with growing enthusiasm and growing pep

With growing vigour and growing energy
Enlightened one be . . with a whole synergy

Passions would reach . . a height too
with growth in harmony
Thus we deduce . . that life is a ceremony

Poem no. 19

David, nicked Dave
Brave Dave

There was a handsome folk named Dave
There was nothing, for which he would crave
All his income was to save
He believed, he was a hunk
In life's tests .. he never flunk
To him, showing off was a waste
He had an elite taste
From life till grave,
a true man in himself ..
.. Dave was really brave
We must thank him for the standards he gave
In his manner, all men must behave

Poem no. 20

Life is Dynamic

We build a vision, we build a foresight
Every morning . . we move towards our smite
An attraction that draws us towards itself
Life could not be decorated on shelf
Life is dynamic . . It moves on
Unsuccessful is the one, who can't carry on
Keeping up with life's pace . . is a talent
That is how we come to know . . if a person is aspirant

Poem no. 21

Life . . a continuous line

Life is not forever
Why moan for feeble dues
Life should teach . . to be clever
Why brood over minor issues
Life is a continuous line, we must catch
before it's gone
Life is something . . we can't have withdrawn

Poem no. 22

A constant Quest

Jumbled up I found . . that life was tricky
The father of creation is certainly need
A constant quest, no one was born lucky
A flame in oneself, God breathes indeed

Poem no. 23

A picture of . . . . Saint !

There will come a time . . when words shall faint
A saturation point . . where statements will have daint
I sketch with my poetry . . a picture of saint
Yet again with words, a story I paint

~ Over ~

perhaps to start again . . !!

I, Janie Yashman, began a journey of words in my poems.
I'm glad that the journey added a good experience to my living, and . .
my existence; adding more value and volume to my life.
I thank my loved ones for their blessings. I thank God !

Poem no. 24

"TEAM REGIME no fun, unless one"

I saw an unfair dream

It took me to an extreme

It made me feel supreme

But it broke, and made me scream

It gave a message, that life isn't always what it may seem

Yet we wait for a golden beam

We come to know life's regime

How may we redeem, unless we form a team

Life is but a dream that makes us experience extreme

Poem no. 25

Maddening Attraction
"INSANE"

I don't understand what was wrong with my brain
There were certain attractions that I could not refrain
All because I chose to walk on a wrong lane
Meaning is simple, words being plain
Much of pain without any gain
I made hell out of my life, I went insane
My mind was without control, a mind I couldn't train
The reason why all my efforts went in vain

Poem no. 26

"STORY . . . of someone similar to me"

There was this gentleman whose name was Shane

His companion was his pet dog; the dog was Great Dane

Similar to me, he was insane

He'd stay lonesome like me, the problem being main

Out of our similarity, I mentioned his name

The only difference being, he could tame

But I wasn't clever enough, I'd rather sink of shame

Poem no. 27

"IMAGINATION... Writer's World"

To me, a wonder world was shown

Where people never sulked or stayed alone

Everyone made merry, their voices had a sweet and melodious tone

The place was such since a heavenly breeze had blown

Yet one wouldn't be curious, where such a world be

Because I'd say, it was a dream to me

A dream . . . full of charisma and amaze

A world I could forever gaze

A place where flair would have been known

Must be a writer's imagination flown

With a imaginative skill. A writer must have grown

A world where no one grew till a crone

It was a dream, realised to be over soon

When it ended, I felt torn

Poem no. 28

"Play of Words"

Simmering golden beam of Sun
Shines and shimmers in its ever frolic fun
Awakens us in a bright way
We feel brand new every day
I'd wish to stay ever merry and sway
That is what I always pray
Through my poetry, my mind I convey
I wish to please the readers, grace and honour them as I may
To me, the most interesting part of it, is the words' play

Poem no. 29

"UNCLE FUN . . . . the ultimate one"

An old folk was called Uncle Fun
He had the wheel of fortune spun
He'd make sure of near perfection
He'd try to be neat in everything he'd have done
His favourite rhyme was 'hot cross bun'
He loved to display warmth and affection
He was a loving and affectionate son
His parents were his inspiration
They were a source of life and energy, like the Sun
Knowledge was his weapon
Words worked for him, like shooting gun . . . that is the story of Uncle Fun
And all about his lifetime stun
He was a unique person
Popular, famous and the ultimate one;
He'd have folks hearts won

Poem no. 30

"The Raging New Breed"

Seeing the progress speed, invoked in them greed

The greed was to be a feed, to those who were in need

The track which they were on, they wondered where it would lead

From a distance, their minds could read

Read the ill intensions, of people with susceptible deed

The people who practiced discrimination, on the basis of colour, caste and creed

Such racists, of which society needed to be freed

The very cause that gave birth to a ragging new breed

The raging new breed is not to humbly plead

Radical in their manner, they have to succeed

Succeed in their mission to pull out corruption seed

They are a promising generation; they can make a change indeed

Yet there remains a big question mark

on how much can they have the masses agreed

Poem no. 31

"If Only One Has a Firm Belief"

Shifting away is no solution.

Self expression is not to conceal.

Let one be heard and understood.

People must speak out about themselves.

They must unveil how they feel.

Experiences are to be shared.

They are to reveal.

Sharing soothes, they bring relief.

It is the way to console.

The way to cure grief

Creativity is the kind of asset that cannot be stolen by a thief

One can create wonders if only one has a firm belief

Poem no. 31

"Gradual Change"

Part I

Step by step one after the other the changes I felt were spiritual

It happened in agreement with a close one

The understanding being mutual

One after another, the incidences made sense

The result being eventual

It all took place slow and steady

Its effect being gradual

Varied were the products as the outcome would differ for each individual

Part II

I didn't want to grow stout nor did I want to shout

All I wished . . . was to shriek out

And delicately disagree with a pout

For things I couldn't do without

Gradually my stress would sprout

I grew into a needy that were what I turned into and became all about

I began resembling an animal with a snout

Poem no. 32

"On a Birthday Dinner"

With emotions so intense; expressions yet simmer

A wonderful family retreat

A lovely event, like a day trimmer

Time froze for a while with my grandmother's ever heart melting smile

This was like a date reminder that in past, I could've been kinder

I dared to observe my mistakes

Noticeable things weren't minor

Moments polished lost glory acting like a chemic shiner

How could I be so mean ever

Understand people that I could never

How could i drag conflicts forever

How could I be such a sinner

I realized it all, on a birthday dinner

I regretted so much, on a birthday dinner

Poem no. 33

"PYGMALION EFFECT"

Affections seek no region, no boundary
Winning a heart is the greatest victory
Confluence of cultures have widened each territory
Horizons have expanded in large symmetry
The world has shrunk . . . with a building up union
Everyone seems to be a healthy companion
Opportunity have risen for every champion
Challenges have broadened their origin and pavilion
Successors follow one another's pathway
Praising each other, the effect is 'Pygmalion

Poem no. 34

"BLINDNESS . . . a deep essence"

The following poetry is not in literal sense
Darkness here, has depth immense
There are feelings that only a blind can sense
The feel of day the night's essence
Some scenic beauty that only a blind can see
The exchange of glimpse from you to me
Next time when you see a blind
Don't think that God has been unkind
God blessed the blind with an extra sense
The blind is at ease while we are tense
This isn't meant in literal sense
Blindness here, is just an essence

Poem no. 35

"FAMILY BUSINESS . . . Morning till Night"

Ever so cheerful Ms. Day knocks the door

First Ms. Morning was lying on the floor

Still sleepy when tea was to pour

Finally awakened schedules were to sure

Like a chirping chick, both the sisters bother till Ms. Evening arrives

This friend of theirs is one who drives

Drives till the long way to Ms. Night

Mr. Sleep snores all the despite

The whole family brings delight

Poem no. 36

"PROBABILITIES . . . hold possibilities"

Life is like a game of dart

One has to play it really smart

Just as a heavy-duty truck

All of us try our luck

It has to be tried very hard

It acts as a safeguard

One cannot afford to retard

Some memories remain scarred

Fortune is certainly barred if we treat it like a plastic card

For every possibility, one must be prepared

There are certain injuries that cannot be repaired

Tanmeyta Darshee Yashman "Darshika"

Poem no. 37

"WHITE AND BLACK"

Last but not the least

The end part is a feast

Vibrations create waves

Yet for one craves

Spirit comes out from their graves

Around us they build their enclaves

Time is what one saves; if properly one behaves

Our ancestors built for us ages

In return, we gift them cages

That is what we lack, when

We see things in white and black

Poem no. 39

"HONEY BEE"

To my sweetheart I wrote

Let's take a ride on a motorboat

To him I sang

When I felt Shut! Slam! Bang!

"You're my bee"

"Honey bee"

"For you I go, week in my knee"

"You're sweet, sweet as honey"

"You buzz around, and take sadness from me"

"Wherever i shall go, whichever place I'd be . . . . I'd think of you coz you're my luck, my

fortune cookie"

"You're my bee . . . honey bee"

Poem no. 40

"JUGGLING, STRUGGLING and SHUFFLING"

Sometimes I'm
"Merry Tanie" ☺
Sweet simply
The other times I'm
"Serious Tanmeyta" B-)
With grace and dignity
But most of the times I'm
"Hyper mad Meya" ^o^
A soul set free
And I keep shuffling between the three

Poem no. 41

"STORY MOVES ON"

From the depth of a long night, broke a fresh dawn
Dawn means a fresh beginning when a dark past is gone
Hi! I'm Janie and I'm back although I was withdrawn
The story moves on
I had to come again. Else I'd be in drain
I'd have been dead. But I preferred to move on instead
That is how I stay ahead
Hi! I'm Janie and I'm back
Back on my original track

Poem no. 43

"Sky" by Tanie

We watch the sun dip gently in the cooling twilight sky
We witness the fire that burns in an evening so shy

We see the faintest trace of stars
We wait for the day's removal of scars

We watch the last hint of fading light
We feel it enclose us within the shadows of the night

Poem no. 44

Tea with me . . Janny
"FREE WILL"

Wherever shall I be,
my loved ones would be the ones, I'd always wish to see
Since I'm the kettle, while they are the tea
Since they are the branches, while I'm their tree
I exercise a will which is free !

Poem no. 45

Fortune Cookie by Clattering Chickie
Speaking Tree with Morning Tea
"POETRY PARROT"

Life smiles, in the blush of dawn

Freshness is felt, in the lush of lawn
History is created, when waste pages are torn
In the lap of danger, a new star is born
Catch me folks, before I'm gone
In ever danger, my life moves on
In my poetry, danger signals warn
That is how I say "Mornie Morn"
(meaning: Good Morning)

Poem no. 46

"She".., Another Me
"AFTER ALL"

Over the years "she" has become a ball
Seems like "she" was meant to fall
'I' am her witness,
From 'my' memories .. her rhymes 'I' recall
'I' seldom give up, 'I' seldom play a doll
"She" was to remain forgotten
"She" has taken birth to get rotten
But 'I' try, like a toddler 'I' crawl
Now 'I' try after all !!

Poem no. 47

Expecting Wishes
"GIFTS"

Evening is gifted, in return for morning
Opportunity is gifted, in return for gambling
Fortune should be gifted, in return for lottery
Wishes must be conveyed, in return for poetry

Poem no. 48

True Intensions of a Flightless Bird
"WITH WORDS SO FEW"

Mornings came chirping to me

Something I felt, was meant to be
As the rockets of messages I blew,
I tried to appeal, with words so few
Dear God, I'm a part of you
Like a bird in the wide open sky, I wish I flew
Into a flightless bird, gradually I grew!
Yet I made an attempt to glide through
My attempt being honest, my intensions being true !!!

Poem no. 49

Visiting Church
"A SPECIAL DAY"

On visiting the church as usual,

dazzling thoughts came up like a jewel

I regret to have ever sounded cruel

I realise of my nature being dual

Every input acted as fuel

In the church, my senseless hatred and useless worries felt washed away

Thus, visiting church is always a special day

Poem no. 50

God's affections still due
for The Rhymes Princess: Tanmeyta Yashman
"NO CLUE"

Dear God, I'm a part of you

Seems all your affections for me, is still due

You've changed from the one I knew

I really repent that my anger flew

I also regret that my hatred blew

It spread like a worthless flu

What exactly agitated me, I have no clue

But I think I shouldn't have kept my brain in my shoe

.. and I must create a scenic view

I must leave a mark of myself, like The Magical Swan

Then would people remember, The Rhymes Princess: Tanmeyta Yashman

Section 2

Fountain of Love

Tanie's Chimes

Hi!

I'm Janie Yashman. I begin a journey of words in this book with a belief that I'd be able to share my experience with worthy people. I thank my well wishers for their blessings.

Above all, I thank divine powers to adorn my book with precious gems of words.

Forever "Janie"

Poem no. 51

Someone Stupid
"SURVIVING"

I'm someone stupid
A drama in myself, I slip and skid
In an auction, my spirit was kept on bid
Yet I'm surviving, like I always did
From ever growing tensions, I had myself hid
Kept leaving each of the course, when the sessions were in mid
My write-ups are all solid,
My desires being valid !!

Poem no. 52

Slice of Life in an Oaf's Loaf
"SMEAR SMITTEN KITTEN"

Although they feel familiar,
yet evoking thoughts are premier
The routes get clearer,
with means that are fairer
"Slice of Life in an Oaf's Loaf"
Tanie, the Oaf
Tanie, the cute kitten . .
clever and yet smear smitten
(smear smitten : smudged in attraction)

Poem no. 53

To God, my best friend, . . I dedicate "POSITIVITY"

Simply for you . . today I write
Just for you . . today I wish I might
I believe that I could try catching my missed flight
Only for you . . today I live
I trust my instincts that I would remain positive

Poem no. 54

Jo, Po, Bless, Dress
"KING BROTHERS FOR SING SISTERS"

Once upon a time there was boy named Jo.

He was the king of laughter, his talent could show

In his memory, we still like joking

And morning times, he liked poking

Jo and Po two brothers a blessing that destiny brings

A child happily sings . . . . the saga of emotional turnings

The child plays guitar of brothers' hearts' strings

In the dressing of bandage, the wound of emotion smiled . . . to be graced with such a

blessing

Bless and dress . . . . two sisters, two angels who sing

Blessing dressing

Jo met Dress and Po met Bless

Angel queens wedlocked fun filled kings

Thus they made a family

Joking is a dressing on sad ones

Poking is a blessing from dear ones

If someone pokes you, you're dear to that person

Bless is so unfortunate,

she creates poetry and stories for an audience that might not have appreciation for it

Yet she finds pleasure in giving her every single bit

The family of four can be felt on a night, moonlit

Poem no. 55

Realising late
"IMMORTAL MATE"

Puzzling is fate

strange are its ways

Realising so late

never understood someone great

Someone who was serving life on plate

A good person is someone who prays,

irrespective of time and date

A pure spirit is someone

who opens victory gate;

someone who could be immortal mate

Poem no. 56

Opposing Forces
"UNEQUALLYEQUAL"

The intelligent Saturn
The intellectual Jupiter
The taste never sweet
The taste never bitter
Velvety violet evenings
and washed white dawns
A conflict between
brains and brawns

Poem no. 57

On the door of day
"MORNING BOY"

A wind of hugging joy
A wink of morning boy
Knocking the door of day
Standing there to say
Let's get movin' douche
Hay!
Time to sing and sway

Poem no. 57

Brooch of Cheer (Part 1)

To someone dear,
a brooch of cheer ~
brings feelings so sheer
Sharing views with peer
Intensions get pure and mind becomes clear
Washed away are needless fear
That is how loved ones come near
Departure from whom, one cant bear

Brooch of Cheer (Part 2)

Let us wear
the brooch of cheer
Tucking good humour
kindliness rests on which
Lively spirits look so dear
Right there,
where heart is near
let us wear, the brooch of cheer

Poem no. 58

The Feeble Ones

Part 1

Just as a new born
worth great care
Soft as petals
Sensitive as dame
Fragile feelings
Feeble little flame
so delicate, so faint
Often like a grandmother
subdued and frail

Part 2

Feelings get hurt
Flame gets blown away
Fertile and expert
Feeble ones pray
They recall God when they feel lack of His attention
They pray for their lives when they seek protection

Poem no. 59

Chasing Mirage

Down the lane
Besides the meadow
I felt a glimpse of gold
I rushed to catch it with fists held tight
and knew that I was bold
The gold was nothing, but a hint of sunbeam
hitting down the open fields
By the time I discovered the fact,
I knew this was something that I'd been told
Grandparents are often correct
with the myths they unfold
They tell us not to chase mirage,
else we'd never grow old

Poem no. 60

A poem from God to a worried Child
"Go STEADY AND SLOW"

Do not dishearten,

be easy and glow

Go steady and slow

Dont grow anxious,

or I'll go

Go steady and slow

Be clever and smart

the way you are,

the way I know

Go steady and slow

And if you fail,

I must not show

Time's like pendulum

moves to and fro

Go steady and slow

You may reep,

as you may sow

Merry times are here to say "Hello"

Now I know,

You'll be a pro

Go steady and slow

Poem no. 61

The unlimited world of Love

Crossing all the boundaries,
it saw no region or belt
People were awestruck and amazed,
realising the limits in which they dwelt
It was the magic of the word Love,
the very moment I had it spelt
It should have awakened us much earlier,
a pleasant surprise I felt

Poem no. 62 (Part 1)

Captivating Sight

We wish we might,
reach the top most height
Then our visions begin to take a flight
when Sun shines lively and bright
and holds us by its captivating sight

(Part 2)

The captivating sight, of a magnificent moonlit night
In a forest with a witch on a boat,
Visions began to take a flight
I kept looking at her, as she rowed
My mind lay on the stream
and I felt I'm to float
My soul rest deep beneath the water
yet I have a heavy throat
Soon I realised that I was sad
but the witch was there to make me feel glad
The witch had once, undergone the same misery
To her, I was a friend with common suffering
In the thicks of forest woods, she began bearing
and gradually disappearing
In my pain where I came running
The pain was tearing
Tearing to the extent ~ that in a witch's arms
I found that I was content

Poem no. 63

Wisdom

Wise is the one who can build a kingdom
Wisdom gives liberty, provides freedom
It can make us reach stardom
It gently removes all the boredom
Wisdom . . . a route to divinity
Wisdom . . . a path of dignity
Wisdom . . . a lifelong journey
Wisdom . . . our very own attorney

Poem no. 64

Passion

Passion ~ the ultimate conquest,
the driving force that makes us feast and fest
Ignited once, hardly at rest
Bringing out hidden skills, builds our nest
A zone where we find comfort,
a home where we are no guest
Turning towards the bests of best
Passion is the feed coming from a motherly breast
Passion allows us to find ourselves,
when we are barely in our twelves
With this note . . . I carry on,
that is how I attest!

Poem no. 65

Difficult Test

Many memories pass me by
as I watch myself long for the surrounding I'd belong the best
Ever since that I've been aware of my senses,
life has been nothing, but a difficult test
It examines my vigour, the endurance to retain my zest

Poem no. 66

Fake approach Survived

In a gloom and betrayal,
the fake approach I survive
Empty, hollow, shallow people come and take a dive
I've been their route, I've been their drive
for I've been vulnerable, I've been naive

Poem no. 67

Part 1

Writing, a friend
In my joys, in my grieves
writing was my friend
It has been a master,
to whom I could bend
It has been an outlet,
wherein my creativity could blend
It has been a gift,
that I could try and send

Part 2

I feel when I was grieved,
my enemies were relieved
My facts were never believed
A past that was retrieved
An ancestral property that I received~
~that was writing, which was deceived

Poem no. 68

A glowing "Good Morning" to say

In the rouge of dawn, in the prelude to day

a sweet promise lay

In the golden ray,

in the currents of gale . .

. . unfolds a lovely tale

There is bound to stay ~

~ many awesome . . . amazing trail

and several opportunities to avail

Love is to replay,

to let harmony prevail

If there be no sign of delay,

one is bound to win without a fail

In the rouge of dawn, in the prelude to day

A blooming bud lay

In a loving manner is conveys . . .

A thoughtful wish it says

"Good Morning"

In the rouge of dawn, in the prelude to day ~

~ a touching wish is felt at heart

The morning arises for a fresh start

Forgotten must be an ill past

One must realise that life is too fast

Poem no. 69

Thoughts, Thoughts, Thoughts

To submerge, thoughts ignite
To survive, thoughts fight
Thinking is Prime,
be it any Time

Poem no. 70

The Change is Now

From a dolphin to a shark
Tearing away the dark
Not to pounce
Not to bark
The change is now
Don't think how
To eternity we bow
Life is like a field we plough
The change is now
Don't think how

Poem no. 71

Everything has a Reason

Whatever we lose, whatever we gain
both hold meaning, both have aim
Victories are bonuses, defeats are lessons
Whether a win or a loss, both have reasons

Poem no. 72

Preach and Pray

Peace in our heart
Worries at the bay
That's how we live
That what we preach and pray
Memories can never be taken away
That's how we rejoice,
we dance and play
We must let go of those who could leave us a stray
and make friends with those who would never betray

Poem no. 73

Lively Weekend

Shining, smiling morning
Bright, joyous day
Nurturing lively weekend
Ooh La La Wow today
Lovely nice times to you
is all I wish to say

Poem no. 74

In Bed, at Night . . "Curl-in time"

Sky is dark
Stars are twinkly
Eyes are dreamy
Mind is sleepy
Soul is mushy
Bed is cushy
Into our bedding . . . we curl-in

Poem no. 75

Cosmic Connection

Our bond with the eternity
. . . a relationship forever
The cosmos and us
. . . bonded ever!!!
We must be prepared, for anything to come
and never say "never"
Only then shall we be . . clever!

Poem no. 76

Destiny . . . . a lesson taught

With sunken heart's fatal attraction,
mind knew that it hardly had an interaction
Moving towards my greatest smite,
that's how every morning I write
In my past birth I'm caught
My present kept me struggling, yet I fought
I realise that my life has become a draught
Hopeless I be, nothing have I got
Destiny is a lesson, which life has taught

Poem no. 77

Memories from Past

Recalling memories from past,
when I had a monitored voice
Feeling good about a few achievements,
I shriek out to rejoice
For following a path made by others,
was never quite my choice

Poem no. 78

Lessons learnt . . . Framing a Wise Thought

Wandering through the day,
I revise what my surrounding taught
Recollecting my scattered spirit,
I remind myself of the battle I fought
Highlighting that each day is a struggle
I deduce that fate cannot be bought
Taking a lonely corner by sunset,
I pen the lessons learnt, to frame a wise thought

Poem no. 79

Allow oneself to see The Best

I see the brightest sides of life,
when I allow myself
I see the darkest sections in living,
when I allow myself
I see the best, not the worst
when I allow myself
I close my eyes and hide in the skies for a while
I open up myself and show on lands with a smile
A lovely life, when I allow myself
A terrific living, when I allow myself

Poem no. 80

Jotting down Thoughts

In the course of day,

I move bit by bit

Gliding through a period,

my expressions turn explicit

By the times sun sets

I take a lonely corner to sit

Jotting down my thoughts,

my ideas begin to split

The courage in heart says,

"never say 'quit!'"

Poem no. 81

The Morning Tea

Arising with the morning tea

A thoughtful time, the morning be

A mind so full

. . full of productivity

A time to come,

filled with activity

The soul held close,

and yet set free

In a careless world,

a place carefree

Arising with . . .

. . the Morning Tea !

Poem no. 82

Desires versus Destiny
Feelings versus Fate

Words are few
Feelings are deep
Hard in reality,
vows to keep
Tough in practicality,
promises to keep
Better off it is . .
. . wastes to sweep
This is called,
a substance leap
Destiny is narrow
Desires are broad
Yet I try
and fight the odd
Fate is hollow
Feelings are deep
Hard are the very,
commitments to keep
Hardships create a vigour
Thus we survive a trigger
Feelings are deep
Expressions are shallow
Desires are broad
Destiny is narrow

Feelings are deep
Fate is hollow
Destiny is narrow
Desires are broad
Life is tough
Yet we fight the odd
Destiny is shallow
Feelings are deep
Dreams may break
and make us weep
Fortune is narrow
Desires are broad
Yet we struggle
and fight the odd!

Poem no. 83

The Story Moves on

From the clouds of a long tale,
Broke a fresh dawn . .
Dawn means a fresh beginning,
when a dark past is gone!
Hello, I'm Tanmeyta "Tanie"
I was withdrawn
Now I'm back
and the story moves on

Poem no. 84

A "Thank You" Poem

To gain all of you back
a delight my heart brings
Thanks for accepting me,
with my mood swings
Sometimes haul
The other times withdrawal
I've been affectionate
I've been upto brawl
Now I cross my palms,
on my knees I crawl
That is how,
I want to thank them all
Those who've been my dear ones,
the ones who've removed my illusions

Poem no. 85

Fight till Discovering Self

Life takes leaps,

jumps left and right

I may be incorrect

I could be right

Till I'm alive,

I've got to fight

Fight my battle,

to discover myself

Then I shall find . .

. . a sunshine bright!

Poem no. 86

Another Promising, Energetic Day

Joyful I watch . . . . the blazing Sunrays

It tears away darkness, I watch with careless gaze

"Welcome another promising, energetic day"

with a cup of tea, granny says

Now I know why . . . . mornings are refreshing always

Each little second,

my dear ones are felt . .

. . from moments of lonliness,

to the times of socialising

My dear ones are felt,

while I keep visualising

. . each little second

Now I know the value . .

. . of friends and family

and the role it plays

Now I know why . . . . my days are refreshing always

Poem no. 87

Sunday

Always there to stay
Cheerful way to play
Rising nice mornings
Happy, pretty day
Full of life Weekend
Woopie Wow Sunday
Heartfelt wishes . .
. . making a lovable holiday

Poem no. 88

Friday

A shine in the eye
with aims for the day
A big wide smile
with best of thoughts to say
A belief in mind
for confidence in every way
Welcome Fame
Welcome Friday

Poem no. 89

Fast Forward and Rewind
"RESTLESS DAME"

In the presence of light,

grow thoughts that ignite

In the absence of same,

gets over . . 'the thinking game'

In the presence of dark,

there kindles a shocking spark

In the absence of same,

mind gets clueless with shame

This reflects the mind of a "Restless Dame"

Mind is poured on a piece of paper, in the form of words

Words of a "Restless Dame"

Whether there be light or there be darkness

. . . . in every situation, there is mindlessness

Mindless one be . . wandering aimless

. . and yet find a mission in the same state of mind

That is the journey of fast forward and rewind!

Poem no. 90

Part 1

Uncovering a Sacred Deal
(by Public Representative)

A day to express, the way I feel
Comes again, for me to reveal
Realities are to be brought up, and no longer to conceal
Unveiling holy truth to uncover a sacred deal
Exposing facts to highlight them, for public appeal
Public's wounds are to heal
Public's wounds must heal

Poem no. 90

Part 2

Challenging a Deal
(by an Elite)

By expressing what I feel
How much I know is to reveal
No longer I shut down or conceal
Seeming violent, I challenge a deal
Without aggression, I make an appeal
I know the way my wounds must heal

Poem no. 91

Angel's Message Indicates Too
"ALMIGHTY's VISION CHASES YOU"

Wherever you go, whatever you do
heavenly eyes follow you
Don't dare to neglect feeble beings
or pay no notice to the ones in need
Angel's message indicates too
Almighty's vision chases you
Divine Messenger points out to . .
. . be aware of what you do
Almighty's vision chases you
Messaging is the medium, God contacts through

Poem no. 92

We Can

We can . . kick problems out,
which is what life's all about
Queries are ever to sprout
One must clear away a doubt
We can . . stir pains round . . with patience
We can . . turn fears down . . with faith
We can . . impress . . with intellect and simplicity
We can . . attract . . with austerity

Poem no. 93

I Love You . . . . For Ever and Ever
"FOREVER FOREVER"

A ray of hope,

goes not ever

A vigour to believe,

makes life clever

I love you . .

forever forever

A conviction so strong,

stays always

A firm belief, never caught by a thief

My trust in you, glows forever

I love you . . for ever and ever

Poem no. 94

Morning Moments

A painting on the canvas of the sky
A view like the bride being shy
Dusted with a pink hue
A scenic beauty, ever so true
The day arises with yet another promise
The morning blossoms like a princess of justice
Our eternal bond with divinity
Our fondness for sovereignty
in the beautiful time of morning
Something that comes without planning
The feel of dew drops on finger tips
The kiss of fresh air on delicate lips
The smell of Earth around
The surrounding spell bound
A lost treasure found
A feel above the ground
We thank each breath we take
We're gratified with each move we make

Poem no. 95

Earn a Praise

In a moonless dawn,
the morning lays
In the lap of rays,
The sunshine plays
To fondle the time,
is my craze
That is the way
of happy days
I frame a phrase
to earn your praise

Poem no. 96

With Faith

With an ambition to grow bigger,
we don't only wish, to earn in figure
We keep waiting for an encouraging trigger
We work upon required vigour
We might leap forward with fright and shiver
Soon with faith, we can remove our quiver
We shall produce, what we wish to deliver

Poem no. 97

Early Morning

It's early morning,
time to leave the bed
Out in the open,
sunlight has spread
Dew drops like pearls,
petals have shed
Babies shall cry,
to have themselves fed
Day awaits with miles to tread
May kind God give us,
our daily bread

Poem no. 98

Work, a Primary Tool

In a hectic life,
with a busy schedule
Muting cheering initiatives,
aims stand like a mule
Rigid kind of, and stubborn,
work is primary tool
Key times pass us by,
forbids us from staying fool

Poem no. 99

Morning Wishes, Served Chilled

The feel of dew,

ever so sheer

The morning time,

is the time to cheer

We recall folks

who are so dear

We commence the day

with a will so clear

One drop of smile

Two of twinkling shine

A full scoop of love

Perfect blend of good wishes, served chilled

Mind swirled with senses spinning

Mischievously, Tanie was grinning

Spinning senses, mind swirled

Tanie says,

"Good Morning World"

Tanie is full of attitude

like a kitten curled

Poem no. 100

Morning . . a Clutch less Time

Early morning, the vibrations are such
They feel like Almighty's healing touch
and tell us, there is still to
explore and experience much
Life is not to be caged
One can't live in a hutch
Freely it moves, life cannot be
Under someone's clutch
Living is all about companionship and dutch

A beautiful journey of words covered and shared with readers, I find satisfaction in
Janie Yashman finds solace in the foam of poetry.
Bubbling thoughts keeps me engaged in a constructive manner.
I, Janie Yashman love to create and share my creations with the ones who're worth it
Once again, I thank God for gracing me with valuable words !

Section 3

Compassionate Wonderland

Tanie's Mimes

Poem no. 101

Strategic Intuition

The complexity of intension
builds a strategic intuition
Life can't stay at suspension
but it's hard to fight inhibition
Clear must be aims and ambition
One must know one's aspiration
There comes again . . strategic intuition

Poem no. 102

Patience
"LIFE TO BREW"

The sky spread out,

ever so blue

A mind reflected,

that must be true

Worries are best,

kept in a shoe

One has to have patience

for life to brew

One has to have patience . . . . for life to brew

Poem no. 103

Good Day

The feel of Dawn
The sky so Blue
A Gentle Breeze . .

. . touches you
They leave a smile,
sparkling on face
With flow of faith . .

. . running through
Together they wish . .
. . a good day too !!

Poem no. 104

Mornings, Noons, Evenings and Nights
"THE DASHING SUN"

The Dashing Sun

speaks again . .

. . the story of ever going life sprites

We must feel the poem that the Dashing Sun recites . .

. . while bringing mornings, noons, evenings and nights !!

Poem no. 105

In Eternity it Lay . .
"TIME"

Time is like pendulum,

to and fro it sway

Time is like sand in palms,

sand slipping away

Time is precious . .

. . in every way

Time is eternal,

in eternity it lay

Time is unpredictable,

no one knows what it has to say

Time is to catch by luck, by chance

everyone wishes they may

Poem no. 106

To My Family I Write
"A LETTER TO MY FAMILY"

Dear Family,

Arms keep yearning

to hug you warm and tight

Eyes keep longing

to see you day and night

Soul keeps desiring

to be ever bright

Mind keeps worrying

That losing family is my greatest fright

I keep telling to myself

that my family is always right

I wish they keep wishing

that I stay in their sight

I keep writing my emotions

to keep my mood light

Sharing my feelings

is ever a delight

Yours Ever

Tanie

Poem no. 107

A Holiday

Go for a bash

or a retreat

All the fun

to repeat

The day rises

with a greet

Holiday comes again

for a treat

Happy Holiday with

a Young Beat

.. A Youthful Beat

On a 'King Size' Seat !!

Poem no. 108

Mornings glow . . . . when You say 'Hie'

Winds blow
Birdies fly
Streams flow
Smiles pass by
Efforts show
when we try
Folks bow . .
. . to a friendly guy
Mornings glow
when pals greet 'hie'
Dear Friend,
If you go,
I would die
Where are you lost

At least reply
Mornings glow
when you say 'hie'

Poem no. 109

Solutions Never Leave us Stray

After a dark night,

comes an encouraging day

After many defeats,

Stands a supportive way

Amidst all the problems,

solutions never leave us stray

Poem no. 110

Zealous Way

Weary nights depart,
arrives a keen day
Losses gradually recover
and assures us of zealous way
Surrounded with difficulties,
enthusiasm makes us pray

Poem no. 111

Luck Cannot be Forced

Talents seek recognition
Abilities need to be endorsed
Given proper ignition,
success could be coursed

Poem no. 112

My Family is My World
"FAMILY IS ALL I'VE GOT"

A constant Quest
to express a thought
Hesitations fought
the anxieties life brought
They'd keep me caught
had I expressed it not
that my family is my world
Family is all I've got

Poem no. 113

Been Stupid

Family grid,
I shouldn't have bid
I repent for what I did
I've been stupid
like an eternal kid
I've been stupid
as a jar without lid
I repent for all the ill I did
I've really been stupid

Poem no. 114

If suddenly I go away
"PARTING FOREVER"

With a pinch to my heart,
I manage to say
'Please don't mind..
.. if suddenly I go away'
'Today could be a parting forever'
This should not bother
as it did not ever
It did never

Poem no. 115

As you Begin a New Journey in Life

As you begin,

a new journey in life,

accept God's blessings

that act as a Guide

A lesson to pass through barriers,

A lesson to glide

for you to commence well

and prevent rife

You're commencing with another angle in life

Heavenly beings are blessing you

May your beginning be like a Rain of Stars

and you never face a strife

Poem no. 116 a

Magical Attraction

I looked at it,
it looked at me
and we were spell bound
For a few moments
that we exchanged our glimpse,
we remained astound
And then we realised,
that the fact remained . .
. . the clock moves round and round
We also observed
that we weren't alone
There were others around
Reaching the stage
where I'd always wish to be,
my heart began to pound
As weird as that,
eccentric I may sound
Yet it is like extracting truth
like a lost treasure found
After feeling the heights of sky,
it is difficult to come back to ground

Poem no. 116 b

Clouds of Love

Clouds of love
so pure and white
Form in sky,
bringing delight
They darken
while feeling hurt and drain
Then rain out
washing all the pain

Poem no. 117

Tricky situation Test our Foolishness

Edges all frayed

leaves one feel delayed

When not being desperate,

adversities eliminate

Tricky tough situation test our foolishness

Test it, to eradicate

Sensitive be a soft feeling

with a mind so delicate

Essence of regale is refreshed

with proper etiquette

Poem no. 118

Happiness

Progress of a dear one
Achievement of an objective to be done
A loved one's heart won
Wishes that a blessing has
A form of God, we could visualise as
Perhaps a tree, that bears the fruit of prosperity
The liveliness in life
The driving force that prevents strife
More than taking, it is about giving
The cause behind care and sharing
The more we chase, the more it hides
It's not a phase, it shifts besides
The glory, the pride
A smiling, blushing bride
Happiness is like a flower
in the garden of satisfaction
It blossoms in the slightest of fraction
Happiness .. a sensitive string
Happiness .. something that close ones can bring
Happiness .. a source of living
Happiness .. a sheer blessing
Sometimes seen, sometimes heard
Happiness is like a bird
Happiness .. It's not just a word !!

Poem no. 119

The Importance of Emotions

Cheerful moments
Times to brood
Polished events
Incidences so crude
Moments of tears
Occasions to smile
Changing period
make us realise for a while
the importance of emotions
throughout our lives, till mind is fertile

Poem no. 120

Gentle Breeze
"DEATH"

After every storm

comes a gentle breeze

The same way

all the emotions are meant to release

Life may not always please

It might scold, it can tease

Yet it moves on, it can't just freeze

That's how we wait . .

. . for a gentle breeze

Sometimes life itself is a storm

and death is breeze

One has to wait . .

. . for a Gentle Breeze

Poem no. 121

Ever Freshness

I felt the ever freshness of wind as I woke
A sweet essence of nature was to evoke
The words of wisdom, gradually I spoke
God seemed like a friend to poke
I felt the ever freshness of wind as I woke

Poem no. 122

Call for The Day . . . . be Hold

It falls on eyes
Feels so warm and comforting
. . the beam of Sun, like Shimmering Gold
It falls over us
Showering its Glare
. . the Call for the Day be hold

Poem no. 123

We try, Yet we don't

Give away dreams
Take away difficulties
We really wish..
.. that we wont
Give up marrying around
Catch up with responsibilities
We try, yet we don't

Poem no. 124

Indian Independence

Without violence or brawl
Equal rights and freedom was set for all
A memory to recall
Years back, our nation went ill
Snatched and ridiculed were common man's skill
Then was ignored foreign rule,
liberation was imparted until
Masses' needs were to fulfil
Suppressed generation was not to kill
Today we celebrate our liberty
We stand on our own, with dignity
After freedom fighters' perspiration,
the country could find emancipation
There was a movement called
Non Cooperation,
that was a kick on British Government's indignation
Otherwise, today how would we find a reason for celebration
Today, how would we define liberation
How would we know what is an independent nation
Duties are the licence to victory
Implementing it, the key to its memory
We must exercise the rights given
We must practice our fundamental duties in order to achieve and retain the liberation
Strugglers' memories must be paid tribute to
From them, we must learn to be honest and true

Tanmeyta Darshee Yashman "Darshika"

This is what the strugglers inspired
Faithful were they, when dishonest people conspired
We must utilize the freedom gifted
We must exploit the conventions shifted
We must make use of Freedom Fighters' inspiration
We must exercise the rights given
Yet prior to this, we must practice our fundamental duties in order to achieve and retain
the liberation
Duties are the licence to victory
Implementing it, is the key to its memory
We must exercise the rights given
We must practice our fundamental duties in order to achieve and retain the liberation

Poem no. 125

Friendship Day

Dear Friend,
When no one does,
you stand by my side . .
You're the one
behind whom I can hide
My wisdom, my joy ride
A holy truth be . .
that you're sacred to me
You're a divine energy
that I can feel and see
A ray of hope
from you to me
Friend, you rock my world
You're a positive vibration
and my inspiration
You fulfill my expectation
You're my gladness,
my grief tOO
You're the one
who knows me thrOUgh . .
Wishes of a happy friendship day
from me to yOU !!
Turn to me, when worries are maNy
Your friend forever . .
JaNie

Poem no. 126

Intelligence Quotient

Circumstances test my ability to strive
Situations check my vigour and drive
I'm someone, who's trying to get
her poems published
Someone who's waiting for her play of words
to be cherished and relished
Someone who is in fact a psychiatry patient
which happened because
of her indigestible intelligence and style quotient
This was because
the audience was either prudish or rubbish
while she, the patient carried a super quarter gene
which is either Swedishly crudish or British
Now don't you think this is like a rap
which sounds funny
Funny enough to earn American money

Poem no. 127

Procreation

Opportunities build a way to revolution
Words make a deep impression
I hope my poetry to have a self expression
Those which come out spontaneously, randomly
without any preparation
I wish they left a long lasting sensation
This is how I sum up creation
This is how I find recreation
This, to me . . . is procreation

Poem no. 128

Rigid Conviction

Wandering in thoughts
became a gradual addiction
Thoughts began to create a friction
Illness became such an infliction
It became difficult
to come out of the formed Rigid Conviction
Facts couldn't win over Fiction

Poem no. 129

Victory of Divine, over the Evil

Vighnaharta is to come

Human agonies are to remove

Vighnaharta is the remover of obstacles,

Lord shall once again prove

Victory of divine over the evil,

Lord shall once again prove

With the holy presence of Ganesha,

all the human conditions are to improve

Lord is waiting to show miracles,

Lord is waiting for us to approve

The remover of obstacles is to come,

darkness and ignorance is to remove

Devotion at the edge,

Worship on the groove

Lord shall show us the way,

a positive direction to move

Vighnaharta is to come,

injustice is to remove

Poem no. 130

Fatherhood

I lift myself up

I learnt it from someone

who had me best understood

I walk my way

On my feet I stood

He made me learn it all

Of course my father, he is

and he gave the best he could

He's a complete man

He fulfilled each criteria of fatherhood

Today on each merit,

I can count upon . .

. . it is my father who showered me all the good

Poem no. 131

The Origin of Complexities

Life went through complexity
Living had undergone complication
but with me, I had a solution to it all
and I knew their implementation
The graces I had with me,
helped me overcome complexities
And on this date I know,
the origin of complexities
It is all set in the mind
if one does not undergo the grind
How could one learn the worth and value of life
when it is gentle and kind

Poem no. 132

Just an Accident

Alas! I could not prevent,
a corrosively damaging event
How could I let it happen,
a future that would have a dent
I kept walking on a risky path,
ignoring my present
Past kept haunting me,
I brood over which and repent
I did not even pay attention,
to my inclinations and natural bent
I wonder if I forgot . . .
that I was prudent
While I willingly prepared myself,
to become a docile student
I guess there was something
which I was trying to invent
And in the process,
I missed to notice my inborn talent
I even took no notice . . .
of the messiahs sent
There are oracles,
to which I'm equivalent
as I remember walking my way
with my guardian's consent
Thus today I feel . . .

that it was correct to walk

on the path that I went

Let me presume everything to be correct,

the rest being . . . just an accident

A wizard's supernatural powers . . .

I'm to represent

Although the wizard might miss an ingredient

The moody wizard shall do whatever convenient

Poem no. 133

Settlement (a sequel to Just an Accident)

It was correct to walk on the path that I went

Let me presume everything to be correct_

the rest being . . just an accident

Jumping to hasty conclusions,

let us not pass a judgement

Why to look onto others' mercy and be dependant

Let me not be worth care as an infant

I should not have a twenty four hours attendant

I've often been hesitant

Things haven't worked for me

with my outlook being reluctant

The reason today I'm left redundant

And yet, a wizard's super natural powers . .

. . I am to represent

This is how we come to a point of agreement

and therefore find a way to settlement

Poem no. 134

Writing .. a Quality Inherent

Writing .. a quality inherent
Writing makes living much coherent
Mind opens up while writing, when more frequent
One writes to seek appreciation and compliment
Writing .. a way to fight situation which is turbulent
Writing .. time effectively spent
Writing .. the way one strives to be excellent
Writing .. one thrives while each time more efficient
Writing .. a good way to fill a mind that's vacant
Writing .. a juice for readers,
a fruit so succulent

Poem no. 135

Communal Harmony

The display of rigidity towards communal tolerance
must be banned at once
People must express affection to one another
and must not raise guns
One must come to reality,
breaking away illusions

Poem no. 136

Gray Matter

The Gray Matter matters,
unless one scatters
Life is served on a platter
if one has Gray Matter
It makes one analyse
In itself, it is a prize

Poem no. 137

A Blessing

Every morning
I like to convey
warm wishes to those
whom I'd wish to gift in every way
It is a blessing to watch loved ones every day
Priceless be their presence
A heart bound emotion to pay

Poem no. 138

Pets . . a Good Company

With fond attachment Pets welcome us
They express their care
Always just, never unfair
Ever open to listening to us,
our feelings they share
Who wouldn't want them
They make with us, a loyal pair
They give a moral boost
They put us on top gear
Fondle plays so sheer, never want to be apart
Always felt near, ever close to heart

Poem no. 139

Teddy Bear

Right there,
where childhood never gets clear
A part of austere
one is to swear
Every girl's favourite toy . .
. . a cuddly teddy bear
No ghosts dare to scare,
The cute teddy toy . . a friend sincere

Poem no. 140

Flaws

Who says flaws are insignificant
They hold their importance
They create a route to substance
How would one speak of perfection
and thus give a chance to correction
Only then can one feel resurrection
Flaws . . not just a clause
Flaws . . till one withdraws

Poem no. 141

Music and Mood

Music creates an appetite
while mood is the feed in itself
Music finds a situation that is just right
and builds a mood to express the self
Music and Mood trigger the inner most soul
Together they both achieve a spiritual goal

Poem no. 142

Clock

Uncle Clock is restless
Let's make him stop ticking for some time
Let's think of a good poem
Let's compose a rhyme
Why not give him a shock
Let's remove the batteries
Let's remove the time's lock
The rest will become a history,
if we let the time not to block
Time never waits for anyone,
no matter how large the stock
Clock . . where moments flock

Poem no. 143

Sincerity

An evidence of concern
A great respect showed in return
Lets no refusal hold it back
Lets no impudence govern
Lets no impoliteness slack
Thus the meaning to Sincerity is to crack

Poem no. 144

Home

The ultimate shelter
A parent in itself
The soul is found where
The key to oneself
A place to let oneself just be
A place to let oneself just flow
The guardian of our spirit
The place which retains our secret
and knows us from every bit
Home . . our very own reflection
Home . . our pinnacle protection
Home . . our only refuge
Home . . could be small or huge

Poem no. 145

On a Birthday Dinner

With sentiments intense;

expressions yet simmer

A wonderful family retreat

A lovely event, like a day trimmer

Time froze for a while

with my grandmother's ever heart melting smile

This was like a date reminder

that in past, I could have been kinder

I dared to observe my mistakes

Noticeable things weren't minor

Moments polished lost glory,

acting like a chemic shiner

How could I be so mean ever

Understand people that I could never

How could I drag conflicts forever

How could I be such a sinner

I realised it all, on a birthday dinner

I regretted so much, on a birthday dinner

Poem no. 146

By a Psychiatrist

What can be a bigger achievement
than learning to ignore the external environment
Be at peace with oneself
because life is not to be decorated on a shelf
What makes a good doctor
that one learns to be a good actor
Specially if the doctor is a psychiatrist
The one who learns to be a fundamentalist
Life is not to babble about
One who does so . . . is chucked out
Why to dabble around
and to be chucked off like ever bound
Once lost, never found
A pinching event, if one ignores
That very moment, vibrancy pours!

Poem no. 147

For Itself

Poetry speaks for itself
lost in nature's embrace
Tranquility speaks for itself
when one can find solace
Elegance speaks for itself in grace
decorating the surrounding with flamboyance
as a flouncy lace
Perfection speaks for itself
without an erroneous trace
Velocity speaks for itself
catching up with life's pace
Confession speaks for itself
when confronted face to face
Solitaire speaks for itself
as each individual deserves a breathing space

Poem no. 148

Comes again, The Grand Day

Comes again . . . the grand day

to wish someone special

I wonder how I may

Long live my love, all I'd say

A sweetheart smiling to this poem

is merry and gay

Glint in her eyes with a streaming ray,

the moment she hears

"many happy returns of the day"

In her smile, eternity lay

May she be blessed with a lively, healthy life;

her dear ones pray

A wishful cake to be served in tray;

to wish someone special . . .

a happy birthday !!

Poem no. 149

How we turn to Our Lord

Life is like that
We wish to bat
Battle against the odd
because every corner has a fraud
This is how we turn to Our Lord
.. the ultimate power, the supreme enery called God

Poem no. 150

My Final Creation
"GUIDE"

To my conviction . . . I feel myself tied

Worldly were the rules . . . by which I couldn't have abide

But I speak the truth . . . I wouldn't have lied

To my heart's content . . . I have cried

Words have evaporated . . . Creativity has dried

Snatched are today . . . my glory and pride

Yet with my enemies . . . I cant have myself allied

I prefer to have myself shut . . . I'd rather hide

or I'd turn to . . . my eternal Guide

Guru ji . . . my mentor, my Guide . . . my glory, my pride

Without whose divine presence . . . I would have died

Author's Biography

Evolved from acute schizophrenic eccentricity, the ever roaming about spirit of the author finds writing poems a way to express the vivid imaginations created in the mind; a medium to reflect the inspirations from the little world around observed keenly; drawing deductions from the natural surrounding and beyond.

A splendid, carefree, wandering soul "Tanmeyta" meaning passionate with only access to the world being TV and Magzines, develops the power to express in words from perceiving and conceiving thoughts via the "media".

Tanmeyta Darshee Yashman ~ nicked Janie, a name given by a worshiped Guru, Pandit Shree Niwas Tiwari ~ nicked Aazaad with the hope to ignite the passion of perceiving and reflecting from the magical world gifted to us all by super natural powers all around us.

The Guru and the devotee belonging to the phenomenally spiritual and mystical lands of Kaashi, once again prove the worth of this cramped appearing town.
The holy, sacred, divine city of Varanasi with its ever charming charisma attracting many known nobles from a fairly known period of time, is the place where the Guru and the devotee come from or are rather representatives of.

Varanasi, one of the oldest living towns in the world known to be birthing many artists and intellectuals since ages.
This extremely fertile city of concepts and perceptions has shaped, formed and built the Guru and the devotee, the writer of this poetry book.

The journey of words begin to add value in the living.

I chase my dreams, locked inside

Smiling sweets times are stored in pride

Pride is in friends and family

Love makes us smile prettily

It's important to love, it's necessary to smile

Smiles confirm of a mind that is fertile

Love can conquor hearts and minds

Love is a crown which a princess finds

Pride is in friends and family

Love makes us smile prettily

It's important to love, it's necessary to smile

Smiles confirm of a mind that is fertile

This beauty that I create, comes from the beauty within me

The beauty of love, love for my family

Life takes leaps, jumps from a point to another

Guides us always, like a caring mother

I could be incorrect, I may be right

As long as I live, I have to fight

Fight my own battle, discover myself

Only then can I find, a sunshine bright

It's important to love, it's necessary to smile

Smiles confirm of a mind that is fertile

Love can conquor hearts and minds

Love is a crown which a princess finds

FMS BHU

Relationships . . , something on which **MANAGEMENT** grips

FMS BHU . . , a family that births **MANAGEMENT GURUS**

FMS BHU . . , where it's all gain and nothing to lose

FMS BHU . . , an institution which bright students chose

FMS BHU . . , a place that intellectuals cannot refuse

FMS BHU . . , where **FINANCES** and **VALUE SYSTEMS** are taught to be reserved

FMS BHU . . , teaches the importance of **PERSONNELS AND ETHICS** to be preserved

OPERATIONS are not to be carried out at the rate of convenience

HUMAN RESOURCES are to be followed with obedience

INFORMATION TECHNOLOGY gives a twitch

MARKETING FUNDAMENTALS act as a stitch

FMS BHU . . , combines it all, making itself rich

The entire **MANAGEMENT STUDIES** rests upon which

Depth in life is brought where

Widened horizons are taught there

FMS BHU . . , where a sharp future generation is built

FMS BHU . . , cheers its students by saying, **"no_regrets,_no_guilt"**

A few more thoughts and rhymes
. . . by Tanie

A dream . . . of my family

Often I think of the good things that life brought to me
Often I feel happy for the nice times which found me worth to be in
Always I see a dream; that is of my family!

Tanmeyta Darshee Yashman "Darshika"

Heartless people said that it was Law

She knocked at every door she saw
and waited for people's hearts to thaw
Still people were rude, they did withdraw
Those heartless ones said that it was Law

Siblings, without a doubt

Away in the distant lands,
a piece of my soul rests.. away
and yet is the one who completes me
The one to whom I belong any time, any day
Away in the distant lands, far from me
. . . someone brightens me more
Someone who frightens my foe
Someone who's mine from head to toe
He's my reflection, or I'm his shadow
He's a need, I can't live without
He's my big brother, with no doubt
When we're together, we chill out
We play, we fight, we scream..
. . we yell, we shout
When we're mushy, we simply pout
There isn't much, I could define about
We're siblings, without a doubt
We celebrate our companionship by shrieking out
We go nuts over one another, we just freak out
Happen may whatsoever,
amongst ourselves . . . we stay devout
We're siblings, without a doubt

Touchy . . Senti . .

Feelings, emotions and sentiments
. . . are like pearls in the thread of warmth . . .
. . . warmth of togetherness,
warmth of care
A closeness to offer, an attachment to share
Sentimental one be . . .
. . . for depth of humanity to see
Thus, this rhyme becomes touchy

Tanie's Fables

The Perfect Land

A Collection of Seven Stories

Fable 1 : <u>Friends and the Fairy</u>

There lived two girls, Anna and Jenny. They were carefree and flicked worries, if any. Their houses were nearby, as they lived in the same colony.

One day, in the park, Anna saw Jenny. Jenny liked Anna, out of children so many. They shook hands and became friends. They taught each other, their styles and trends. Gradually, they appeared like twins. It was just like destiny wins.

One fine day an Angel was passing by the park. It was late in the evening and quite dark. Yet she caught a glimpse of the two divine friends. She felt like their guardian, the one God sends.

Friends were surprised when the fairy came to them. She hugged them both and gifted them a heart shaped gem. She told them that they've been rewarded for their affectionate bond. The gem was a token of their friendship and beyond.

Soon the fairy flew up high in the sky, then bid girls a sweet goodbye. The friends were still awe struck in surprise; they were very happy with their unexpected prize. They vowed to keep the token safe, in a lock. They felt blessed and confirmed that their friendship was to ever rock.

Every morning, from behind the Sun, they saw Mother Angel waving them and wishing them all fun.

<u>Moral</u> – "Angels bless good friends"

Fable 2 : <u>Girl with a dolly and a doggy</u>

Once upon a time, there was a girl named Tily. She was known to be funny and silly. She carried her doll along with her, wherever she went: like it was a charm specially sent. Her doggy also followed her most of the times. Doggy wished to safeguard her from rising crimes.

People knew Tily as someone crazy. She was also known to be fickle and lazy. Her doll became a symbol of madness: but Tily saw it as a token of gladness.

At a point of time there struck sorrow and gloom in the enclave where Tily lived. Tily was the one who never cribbed. She was merry as she always used to be . . . ever was: because she never lived on rules or laws. She was such a sketch that Almighty draws. She was splendid with no claims or clause. Her life was to move on without a pause.

As we know that Tily's ever lucky companions were doggy and dolly: she was content with them from the time she was a baby crawly.

Gradually people understood what their significance meant. A priest explained them in a Church where they went. They were taught how life was supposed to be spent. When everyone was wrong, only Tily was right. That is the reason why Tily was ever bright.

<u>Moral</u> - "lonesome people must not be under-estimated"

Fable 3 : <u>Gentle Guidance removes Prudence</u>

Poor little Hannah was prude. Over minor issues she would brood. She never meant to be mean, but appeared rude.

Hannah had a brother. He was seven years older. His name was Henry and his attitude was much better. He was really very different from his sister. He was more cheerful than her.

People found Henry, totally contrast of Hannah, in every manner. Henry was known to be Hannah's opposite. With a friendly outlook and generous approach, his demeanours being exquisite.

Out of all the difference which Henry shared with his beloved little sister, he still cared, more than a lot, about her. No one could feel Hannah's innocence but Henry understood. This is the reason he thanked the charmed hood. It was sold by a magical spirit which was passing by with a wand and wood. The hood was working wonders, making Hannah the way a prayer should. Henry was happy with the results and grateful to the spirit as he ever would. Henry's wish was honest and thus the outcome was good. Henry was keen with his patience in itself a wonder. With his lovely sister, he never made a blunder.

Hannah was gently taken care of, by her motherly brother, for a long while. She began to wear a sweet smile. Henry was filled with delight and pride. He learnt that he was a successful guard and guide. He expected Hannah to leap with stride and feel like a bird above the clouds, like those who glide. Henry waited for the day when he could see in the form a beautiful bride.

One day while playing with Hannah in a lush lawn, he observed his sister's rashness to be gone. She was trying to leave her worries aside; she made an attempt to move on.

Henry was able to change his sister's image. He could soothe her wounds and calm her down as well as her growing rage. Among many girls of her age, soon Hannah was able to camouflage.

The lady never returned: the one who was a passing spirit. It seemed that she was Henry's and Hannah's mother, who perhaps was worried a bit. But she had faith in Henry, her capable son: that with his strong will, everything would be well done.

<u>Moral</u> - "With faith, patience and a gentle approach, even difficult people can be managed"

Fable 4 : <u>Elizabeth with her Mystical hat and Kitty Cat</u>

Elizabeth enjoyed a life free of rush. For her, worldly thoughts were all a waste to flush. Gardens would welcome her with its soothing lush. Compliments for her beauty, would make her blush. Elizabeth's dreams were all high. Without her dreams, she would die. But confident she was and never to sigh. She was honest about her goals, for never would she lie. Her whims were named "American Pie".

Wiccan was Elizabeth, her nick was Lizzie. She was fond of her cat named Kitty. Lizzie and kitty, both were pretty. Lizzie would humour around, she was really witty. Kitty would be a tool to inspire; it made Lizzie to try her best and aspire. Lizzie wished to progress and reach up higher, yet never would she want an apprentice to hire. Lizzie was to be a perfectionist and her needs seemed dire. Lizzie also wore her grandmum's hat sometimes; which made her write spells and rhymes. Lizzie would completely change her attire. She did so, secretively and yet worth admire.

The hat was known as "the thinking hat" of the wiccans. It was a device by which weariness shuns. Shunning away useless worries, that is how trash buries.

Lizzie wore her hat on weekends. It made her aware who was real and who pretends. Lizzie appeared ghostly, as the cat kept her accompanied mostly.

Clever Lizzie created a mysticism that no one dare. It was her style, not meant to scare. Wiccan practice was Lizzie's natural flair. She discovered magical powers, layer after layer. Every spell was like a prayer. Lizzie used them often, but they weren't meant to share. She was religious about her spells and never unfair. This kept her on ever top gear. It was a sacred energy, that was rare. She stored the spells with all the care. It was like ancestral property never meant to bare.

Lizzie accomplished all her tasks well. She learnt it from a magical spell. About her wiccan living, she was not to tell. With humanly society, she couldn't ever gel. She switched to a usual person, whenever rang her doorbell. Tragically, Lizzie remained limited to her personal spell. She had a home with a witchy smell.

Later what happened remains a mystery. The rest was a surprising history. Lizzie retained her forbidden ancestry. In her remembrance, wiccans still keep a token of her home's tapestry.

Lizzie is remembered as a fine witch. Her place in the Wiccan history, no one could switch. Lizzie is paid tribute by the wiccans and no one has ever been able to be as rich.

Moral - ": All witches are not harmful to people. It is just that they like their mystical living "

Fable 5 : <u>Sob transformed into a Throb . . a heart-throb</u>

Bob and Benny worked in an office. They worked in a team with an environment free of malice. Bob was lean while Benny was stout. Both worked in peace and never did they shout. Yet, often Benny would feel guilty to see Bob's pout: as Bob would only do so, when he'd feel left out. Bob felt low, since Benny was always a step above, while he was below.

Benny was frisky. He liked to take up endeavours that were risky. Benny would chirp around, while Bob would hardly create a sound.

One day, came the boss named Eric. To him, Benny played a trick and showed his skill to be really quick. Boss was impressed, but he found Bob depressed. He asked him the reason to feel so suppressed.

Eric and Benny decided to brighten Bob. They were to change the angle of his mood's knob. Bob was often misunderstood as snob, while in reality, he'd keep efforting to prevent any sort of mob. It was high time that from Benny, he got a lob.

Benny was a sweetheart of everyone. People helped him in whatever he asked to be done. He asked people to cheer up Bob forever. Everyone wanted Bob to be clever. They expected more zest in his endeavour.

Bob co operated with them to get enlightened. Gradually people never saw him disheartened. This is how Bob was brightened. He was to open up with people and no longer stay frightened. Bob had remained blue, although from within, he was true. Benny understood him and never had an attitude of "dude, you remain stupid, it's not my prob!" With Benny, Bob too became a throb and never again, was he to sob. A talent he gained, that no one could rob. Benny was the best, at this job.

<u>Moral</u> - "Dull people can be brought to life. It's possible"

Fable 6 : <u>Glory of Dignity</u>

On a flowery fresh day, began a story. This was the story of pride and glory. Children celebrated their unity with stride. On a bridge of rainbow, they had a sunshine ride.

One fine day, came Uncle Loy. They, the children, jumped out of joy. Uncle Loy was like their teddy bear toy. He was round and stout – a big fat boy. Uncle told the kiddies, rhymes and riddles, whole day they made merry, with chuckling giggles.

Laughing and playing, they spent their days, on a lush green lawn. Carefree they laze and moved on. Yet, the real story is still to come. Difficult time was to wisely overcome.

One bully came to bother their uncle. He was rounder and fatter than uncle himself. Children were worried and didn't know what to do. They prayed to God to learn a trick or two. Soon they were able to flick the bully away. With reborn happiness, they made their way. They realised the power of their unity and promised each other to retain their integrity.

This is the actual moral of the story: dignity is pride: dignity is glory. Dignity lives in unity and integrity.

<u>Moral</u> – "Dignity lives in unity and integrity"

The Perfect Land Poetry

Tears weren't ever shown

Sorrow was never known

Where Sun happily shone

Folks were merry bone

They spoke in a melodious tone

To a great maturity they had grown

No one was to groan, moan or mourn

No one aged until a crone

No one left one another alone

The reason no one was accident prone

People avoided loan

To God they had it sworn

Blessed were they borne

Blessed were they borne

Story of a Perfect Land to follow . . . .

Fable 7 : <u>The Perfect Land</u>

Tom lived with his mom. There prevailed calm, where they came from. Never ever hit there, devastating storm. The surrounding was always serene and warm. Mornings like Easter and evenings as Prom. No customs to follow, not a single norm. Everything was shared and exchanged. Nothing was bought or sold. That is what my grandfather told. People were humble, never too bold. That is how, they never grew old.

Tommy and mommy lived happily with each other. They had immense regard for one another. Mommy was a great mother. Her nature was gentle as a feather. So soft and light hearted she'd be, yet ever changing and dynamic as a passing weather. A sparkle in her gestures, with twinkly eyes forever. Her name was sweet as her, she was called Heather.

Heather and Tommy made cookies for children's "cookie bank". The children helped setting it up with wooden plank. In reward for their goodwill, an air of praise they drank. They'd always be merry and never stay blank.

Children were well behaved round the clock. Their capabilities were to show and never at lock. Every evening, at park they'd flock. Never for their parents, did they create a shock. Nor towards animals or elders, did they attempt to mock. All of them intended to form a good stock.

Early morning, before sunrise they woke. When they woke up, their foreheads their mommies would stroke. The dawn would appear misty as smoke. A cute picture of the beautiful countryside would evoke. How amazing the village be . . . how nice each of the folk. It seemed they'd shower honey, when they spoke. For fun and laughter, they'd merrily poke.

With its charm, a dreamland it felt. Minds were at breeze and hearts were to melt. A perfect country it was, where Tommy and mommy dwelt.

People never acted pricey or proud. They were soft spoken and never spoke loud. The countryside seemed like a distinct place, under the shade of an exclusive cloud. To such a village, everyone bowed.

Minds like breeze. There was nothing to tease. Everyone would ever stay at ease. To one another, each one would please. Emotions flowed; and simmering life glowed.

Moral - "Love, warmth, affections for one another and good behaviour makes a perfect land"

A poem to compliment the moral of the story

Warmth and Affections

Late in the evening, yesterday,

as I went in the wide open space to pray . .

. . a spiritually awakening wind blew . .

. . enveloping me, it touched me through

On me, a reflection it threw

Its motive so pure and intensions so true

Honest objectives had my thoughts flew

I felt it trying to heal my blue

Late in the evening, yesterday,

as I went in the wide open space to pray

Warm and affectionate wind was blowing

With emotions and sentiments, it was flowing

Late in the evening, yesterday,

as I went in the wide open space to pray

I could sense my mind cry . .

. . as the waves passed me by

I tried to hear the wind, on my way

Tanmeyta Darshee Yashman "Darshika"

Way back to home, where I'd belong . . . . as I may

Late in the evening, yesterday,

as I went in the wide open space to pray

I could sense the waves speak

Ancestral information was to leak

"Brotherhood removes barriers, warmth and affections are the carriers

With friendship, world can be won

Hatred be removed, sins undone

Good relationships overcome fuss

Our forefathers built it for us!"

Late in the evening, yesterday as I went in wide open space to pray

I could feel the waves around me say

The waves created a new ray

Ray of hopes, as it may

I felt the message it had to convey

"Be like me, warm and affectionate"

I could feel it say!

In their remembrance, a tribute we must pay

I really could feel the winds say

Late in the evening, yesterday,

as I went in the wide open space to pray

Tanie's Fables Over